The Rose

By

William Butler Yeats

with a Foreword and Postscript

by Tim Dalgleish

The Rose first published in 1893

Foreword to *The Rose*
Copyright © 2016
The moral right of the author has been asserted.
All rights reserved. No part of this introduction may be reproduced, distributed or transmitted in any form or by any means (including photocopying, recording or other electronic or mechanical methods) without the prior written permission of both the copyright owner and the publisher, except in the case of brief quotations embodied in critical reviews and certain non-commercial uses permitted by copyright law. For permission requests contact the author at lookingfortim.com

The Rose also available as an audiobook
(from Amazon-Audible)
read by
Tim Dalgleish

'Sero te amavi, Pulchritudo tam antiqua et tam nova! Sero te amavi.'

SAINT AUGUSTINE

DEDICATION

To Lionel Johnson

CONTENTS

Foreword	9
The Rose Upon the Rood of Time	13
Fergus and The Druid	14
The Death of Cuchulain	16
The Rose of the World	20
The Rose of Peace	21
The Rose of Battle	22
A Faery Song	24
The Lake Isle of Innisfree	25
A Cradle Song	26
A Song of the Old Mother	27
The Pity of Love	28
The Sorrow of Love	29
When You are Old	30
The White Birds	31
A Dream of Death	32
A Dream of a Blessed Spirit	33
The Man Who Dreamed of Faeryland	34

The Two Trees	36
To Ireland in the Coming Times	38
Postscript: WB Yeats and Today's Political Elite	40
About the Author & Editor	48

ACKNOWLEDGMENTS

The editor would just like to add his thanks to Eamonn Dolan and Carabosse Theatre Company for introducing him to the poem *The Lake Isle of Innisfree* and indirectly inspiring the creation of this work and the audiobook version. His love for his wonky family has also made the production of the book, as ever, a delight in a cold office.

Foreword

If you love poetry, you can love the poetry of William Butler Yeats. A little patience brings great reward, and the poems will *'wrap you round'* if you let them.

Yeats was a man of many dimensions, and literary personae and a certain fear can be instilled by this reputation in the potential reader. It was not for no reason that Richard Ellmann subtitled his famous biography, *The Man and the Masks* but like all the best poetry, one can enjoy Yeats' poetic gift without knowing anything of the man who wrote the poetry or his mythopoetic endeavours and subterfuges. I believe if you read, and re-read, the poems in this collection, their depth, beauty, romance, and brilliance will shine through into the heart of any reader and *'light up your russet brow.'*

The Rose was the second collection of poetry from a young man who was full of the romance of his native country. In 1893, when *The Rose* was published, Yeats was a member of the Gaelic league, but like many proto-political Irish nationalists, he was hardly expecting the storm that arrived in 1916. His poetry, at this time, was symbolic, apolitical and he was content to write, as he says in the opening poem of the collection, in English, rather than *'chaunt a tongue*

[Gaelic] that men do not know.'

Yeats uses the image of the rose to symbolize a number of different things within the collection. Perhaps the most private reference is to Maud Gonne, his great unrequited love, whom he corresponded with almost his entire life, from the age of 23 to his death in 1939. She, who was politically, the more active nationalist, was his dark rose: thorny, untouchable, beautiful. The rose, more obviously, stands for Ireland itself, indeed in Irish mythology, Ireland or Eire is often referred to as the *'Roisin Dubh'* or *'dark rose'*.

Whether one knows the mythology of Ireland or not, one can enjoy Yeats' poems because it is self-evident that the poet knows the myths from the inside. Root and flower, scent, and symbolic petal decorate his interior self, and this communicates and translates itself, powerfully and imaginatively, into the psyche of the reader. One need not have ever heard of Cuchulainn before, to know he is a great and mythical leader of the Irish. One need not know, that at seventeen, Cuchulainn defended Ulster from Mebt, the raiding queen of Connacht, who had planned to steal the great stud bull, Donn Cuailnge, to recognize that Yeats is drawing from a rich mythological earth of tales long told. Cuchulainn, his wife Emer, Conchubar his uncle, Usna, Conchubar's wife and Fergus, Cuchulainn's great rival, all have that gravitas on the page that is pungent, remarkable and ancient.

The collection also contains one of Yeats' most famous poems, *The Lake Isle of Innisfree* which is rightly famous and stands alone in the sea of poetry perfectly happily, without reference to the rest of the collection. But for the poet, often the poems of a collection are borne into the world, with the intention that they be read together, so as to cross-fertilize and for the seed of one poem to blow through the air of another. The truth is *The Lake Isle of Innisfree* was planted amongst the other 'roses' of this collection, as one of many, to colour and make fragrant, our dreams; *The Rose*, is a unified complex of poetry, a collection, a vessel, a bag, it's symbolic petals and thorns were, and are, for the *'pilgrim soul in you'*. As the aged Druid says to Fergus,

'Take… this little bag of dreams;
Unloose the cord, and they will wrap you round'.

Note to second edition
I have made some very minor corrections to the text and included the essay *WB Yeats and Today's Political Elite* as a postscript.

TO THE ROSE UPON THE ROOD OF TIME

Red Rose, proud Rose, sad Rose of all my days!
Come near me, while I sing the ancient ways:
Cuchulain battling with the bitter tide;
The Druid, gray, wood-nurtured, quiet-eyed,
Who cast round Fergus dreams, and ruin untold;
And thine own sadness, whereof stars, grown old
In dancing silver-sandalled on the sea,
Sing in their high and lonely melody.
Come near, that no more blinded by man's fate,
I find under the boughs of love and hate,
In all poor foolish things that live a day,
Eternal beauty wandering on her way.

Come near, come near, come near—Ah, leave me still
A little space for the rose-breath to fill!
Lest I no more hear common things that crave;
The weak worm hiding down in its small cave,
The field mouse running by me in the grass,
And heavy mortal hopes that toil and pass;
But seek alone to hear the strange things said
By God to the bright hearts of those long dead,
And learn to chaunt a tongue men do not know.
Come near; I would, before my time to go,
Sing of old Eire and the ancient ways:
Red Rose, proud Rose, sad Rose of all my days.

FERGUS AND THE DRUID

FERGUS.
THE whole day have I followed in the rocks,
And you have changed and flowed from shape to shape.
First as a raven on whose ancient wings
Scarcely a feather lingered, then you seemed
A weasel moving on from stone to stone,
And now at last you wear a human shape,
A thin gray man half lost in gathering night.

DRUID.
What would you, king of the proud Red Branch kings?

FERGUS.
This would I say, most wise of living souls:
Young subtle Conchubar sat close by me
When I gave judgment, and his words were wise,
And what to me was burden without end
To him seemed easy, so I laid the crown
Upon his head to cast away my care.

DRUID.
What would you, king of the proud Red Branch kings?

FERGUS.
I feast amid my people on the hill,
And pace the woods, and drive my chariot wheels
In the white border of the murmuring sea;
And still I feel the crown upon my head.

DRUID.
What would you, king of the proud Red Branch kings?

FERGUS.

I'd put away the foolish might of a king,
But learn the dreaming wisdom that is yours.

DRUID.
Look on my thin gray hair and hollow cheeks,
And on these hands that may not lift the sword,
This body trembling like a wind-blown reed.
No maiden loves me, no man seeks my help,
Because I be not of the things I dream.

FERGUS.
A wild and foolish labourer is a king,
To do and do and do, and never dream.

DRUID.
Take, if you must, this little bag of dreams;
Unloose the cord, and they will wrap you round.

FERGUS.
I see my life go dripping like a stream
From change to change; I have been many things,
A green drop in the surge, a gleam of light
Upon a sword, a fir-tree on a hill,
An old slave grinding at a heavy quern,
A king sitting upon a chair of gold,
And all these things were wonderful and great;
But now I have grown nothing, being all,
And the whole world weighs down upon my heart:
Ah! Druid, Druid, how great webs of sorrow
Lay hidden in the small slate-coloured thing!

THE DEATH OF CUCHULAIN

A man came slowly from the setting sun,
To Forgail's daughter, Emer, in her dun,
And found her dyeing cloth with subtle care,
And said, casting aside his draggled hair:
'I am Aleel, the swineherd, whom you bid
Go dwell upon the sea cliffs, vapour-hid;
But now my years of watching are no more.'

Then Emer cast the web upon the floor,
And stretching out her arms, red with the dye,
Parted her lips with a loud sudden cry.

Looking on her, Aleel, the swineherd, said:
'Not any god alive, nor mortal dead,
Has slain so mighty armies, so great kings,
Nor won the gold that now Cuchulain brings.'

'Why do you tremble thus from feet to crown?'

Aleel, the swineherd, wept and cast him down
Upon the web-heaped floor, and thus his word:
'With him is one sweet-throated like a bird,
And lovelier than the moon upon the sea;
He made for her an army cease to be.'

'Who bade you tell these things?' and then she cried
To those about, 'Beat him with thongs of hide
And drive him from the door.' And thus it was;
And where her son, Finmole, on the smooth grass
Was driving cattle, came she with swift feet,
And called out to him, 'Son, it is not meet
That you stay idling here with flocks and herds.'

'I have long waited, mother, for those words;
But wherefore now?'

'There is a man to die;
You have the heaviest arm under the sky.'

'My father dwells among the sea-worn bands,
And breaks the ridge of battle with his hands.'

'Nay, you are taller than Cuchulain, son.'

'He is the mightiest man in ship or dun.'

'Nay, he is old and sad with many wars,
And weary of the crash of battle cars.'

'I only ask what way my journey lies,
For God, who made you bitter, made you wise.'

'The Red Branch kings a tireless banquet keep,
Where the sun falls into the Western deep.
Go there, and dwell on the green forest rim;
But tell alone your name and house to him
Whose blade compels, and bid them send you one
Who has a like vow from their triple dun.'

Between the lavish shelter of a wood
And the gray tide, the Red Branch multitude
Feasted, and with them old Cuchulain dwelt,
And his young dear one close beside him knelt,
And gazed upon the wisdom of his eyes,
More mournful than the depth of starry skies,
And pondered on the wonder of his days;
And all around the harp-string told his praise,
And Conchubar, the Red Branch king of kings,
With his own fingers touched the brazen strings.

At last Cuchulain spake, 'A young man strays
Driving the deer along the woody ways.
I often hear him singing to and fro;
I often hear the sweet sound of his bow,
Seek out what man he is.'

One went and came.
'He bade me let all know he gives his name
At the sword point, and bade me bring him one
Who had a like vow from our triple dun.'

'I only of the Red Branch hosted now,'
Cuchulain cried, 'have made and keep that vow.'

After short fighting in the leafy shade,
He spake to the young man, 'Is there no maid
Who loves you, no white arms to wrap you round,
Or do you long for the dim sleepy ground,
That you come here to meet this ancient sword?'

'The dooms of men are in God's hidden hoard.'

'Your head a while seemed like a woman's head
That I loved once.'

Again the fighting sped,
But now the war rage in Cuchulain woke,
And through the other's shield his long blade broke,
And pierced him.

'Speak before your breath is done.'

'I am Finmole, mighty Cuchulain's son.'

'I put you from your pain. I can no more.'

While day its burden on to evening bore,

With head bowed on his knees Cuchulain stayed;
Then Conchubar sent that sweet-throated maid,
And she, to win him, his gray hair caressed;
In vain her arms, in vain her soft white breast.
Then Conchubar, the subtlest of all men,
Ranking his Druids round him ten by ten,
Spake thus, 'Cuchulain will dwell there and brood
For three days more in dreadful quietude,
And then arise, and raving slay us all.
Go, cast on him delusions magical,
That he may fight the waves of the loud sea.'
And ten by ten under a quicken tree,
The Druids chaunted, swaying in their hands
Tall wands of alder and white quicken wands.

In three days' time, Cuchulain with a moan
Stood up, and came to the long sands alone:
For four days warred he with the bitter tide;
And the waves flowed above him, and he died.

THE ROSE OF THE WORLD

Who dreamed that beauty passes like a dream?
For these red lips, with all their mournful pride,
Mournful that no new wonder may betide,
Troy passed away in one high funeral gleam,
And Usna's children died.

We and the labouring world are passing by:
Amid men's souls, that waver and give place,
Like the pale waters in their wintry race,
Under the passing stars, foam of the sky,
Lives on this lonely face.

Bow down, archangels, in your dim abode:
Before you were, or any hearts to beat,
Weary and kind one lingered by His seat;
He made the world to be a grassy road
Before her wandering feet.

THE ROSE OF PEACE

IF Michael, leader of God's host
When Heaven and Hell are met,
Looked down on you from Heaven's door-post
He would his deeds forget.

Brooding no more upon God's wars
In his Divine homestead,
He would go weave out of the stars
A chaplet for your head.

And all folk seeing him bow down,
And white stars tell your praise,
Would come at last to God's great town,
Led on by gentle ways;

And God would bid His warfare cease,
Saying all things were well;
And softly make a rosy peace,
A peace of Heaven with Hell.

THE ROSE OF BATTLE

Rose of all Roses, Rose of all the World!
The tall thought-woven sails, that flap unfurled
Above the tide of hours, trouble the air,
And God's bell buoyed to be the water's care;
While hushed from fear, or loud with hope, a band
With blown, spray-dabbled hair gather at hand.
Turn if you may from battles never done,
I call, as they go by me one by one,
Danger no refuge holds, and war no peace,
For him who hears love sing and never cease,
Beside her clean-swept hearth, her quiet shade:
But gather all for whom no love hath made
A woven silence, or but came to cast
A song into the air, and singing past
To smile on the pale dawn; and gather you
Who have sought more than is in rain or dew
Or in the sun and moon, or on the earth,
Or sighs amid the wandering, starry mirth,
Or comes in laughter from the sea's sad lips;
And wage God's battles in the long gray ships.
The sad, the lonely, the insatiable,
To these Old Night shall all her mystery tell;
God's bell has claimed them by the little cry
Of their sad hearts, that may not live nor die.

Rose of all Roses, Rose of all the World!
You, too, have come where the dim tides are hurled
Upon the wharves of sorrow, and heard ring
The bell that calls us on; the sweet far thing.
Beauty grown sad with its eternity
Made you of us, and of the dim gray sea.

Our long ships loose thought-woven sails and wait,
For God has bid them share an equal fate;
And when at last defeated in His wars,
They have gone down under the same white stars,
We shall no longer hear the little cry
Of our sad hearts, that may not live nor die.

A FAERY SONG

*Sung by the people of faery over Diarmuid and Grania, who
lay in their bridal sleep under a Cromlech.*

We who are old, old and gay,
O so old!
Thousands of years, thousands of years,
If all were told:

Give to these children, new from the world,
Silence and love;
And the long dew-dropping hours of the night,
And the stars above:

Give to these children, new from the world,
Rest far from men.
Is anything better, anything better?
Tell us it then:

Us who are old, old and gay,
O so old!
Thousands of years, thousands of years,
If all were told.

THE LAKE ISLE OF INNISFREE

I will arise and go now, and go to Innisfree,
And a small cabin build there, of clay and wattles made;
Nine bean rows will I have there, a hive for the honey bee,
And live alone in the bee-loud glade.

And I shall have some peace there, for peace comes dropping slow,
Dropping from the veils of the morning to where the cricket sings;
There midnight's all a glimmer, and noon a purple glow,
And evening full of the linnet's wings.

I will arise and go now, for always night and day
I hear lake water lapping with low sounds by the shore;
While I stand on the roadway, or on the pavements gray,
I hear it in the deep heart's core.

A CRADLE SONG

The angels are stooping
Above your bed;
They weary of trooping
With the whimpering dead.

God's laughing in heaven
To see you so good;
The shining Seven
Are gay with His mood.

I kiss you and kiss you,
My pigeon, my own;
Ah, how I shall miss you
When you have grown.

THE SONG OF THE OLD MOTHER

I rise in the dawn, and I kneel and blow
Till the seed of the fire flicker and glow;
And then I must scrub and bake and sweep
Till stars are beginning to blink and peep;
And the young lie long and dream in their bed
Of the matching of ribbons for bosom and head,
And their day goes over in idleness,
And they sigh if the wind but lift a tress:
While I must work because I am old,
And the seed of the fire gets feeble and cold.

THE PITY OF LOVE

A pity beyond all telling
Is hid in the heart of love:
The folk who are buying and selling;
The clouds on their journey above;
The cold wet winds ever blowing;
And the shadowy hazel grove
Where mouse-gray waters are flowing
Threaten the head that I love.

THE SORROW OF LOVE

The quarrel of the sparrows in the eaves,
The full round moon and the star-laden sky,
And the loud song of the ever-singing leaves,
Had hid away earth's old and weary cry.

And then you came with those red mournful lips,
And with you came the whole of the world's tears,
And all the trouble of her labouring ships,
And all the trouble of her myriad years.

And now the sparrows warring in the eaves,
The curd-pale moon, the white stars in the sky,
And the loud chaunting of the unquiet leaves,
Are shaken with earth's old and weary cry.

WHEN YOU ARE OLD

When you are old and gray and full of sleep,
And nodding by the fire, take down this book,
And slowly read, and dream of the soft look
Your eyes had once, and of their shadows deep;

How many loved your moments of glad grace,
And loved your beauty with love false or true;
But one man loved the pilgrim soul in you,
And loved the sorrows of your changing face.

And bending down beside the glowing bars
Murmur, a little sadly, how love fled
And paced upon the mountains overhead
And hid his face amid a crowd of stars.

THE WHITE BIRDS

I would that we were, my beloved, white birds on the foam of the sea!
We tire of the flame of the meteor, before it can fade and flee;
And the flame of the blue star of twilight, hung low on the rim of the sky,
Has awaked in our hearts, my beloved, a sadness that may not die.

A weariness comes from those dreamers, dew-dabbled, the lily and rose;
Ah, dream not of them, my beloved, the flame of the meteor that goes,
Or the flame of the blue star that lingers hung low in the fall of the dew:
For I would we were changed to white birds on the wandering foam: I and you!

I am haunted by numberless islands, and many a Danaan shore,
Where Time would surely forget us, and Sorrow come near us no more;
Soon far from the rose and the lily, and fret of the flames would we be,
Were we only white birds, my beloved, buoyed out on the foam of the sea!

A DREAM OF DEATH

I dreamed that one had died in a strange place
Near no accustomed hand:
And they had nailed the boards above her face,
The peasants of that land,
And, wondering, planted by her solitude
A cypress and a yew:
I came, and wrote upon a cross of wood,
Man had no more to do:
She was more beautiful than thy first love,
This lady by the trees:
And gazed upon the mournful stars above,
And heard the mournful breeze.

A DREAM OF A BLESSED SPIRIT

All the heavy days are over;
Leave the body's coloured pride
Underneath the grass and clover,
With the feet laid side by side.

One with her are mirth and duty;
Bear the gold embroidered dress,
For she needs not her sad beauty,
To the scented oaken press.

Hers the kiss of Mother Mary,
The long hair is on her face;
Still she goes with footsteps wary,
Full of earth's old timid grace.

With white feet of angels seven
Her white feet go glimmering;
And above the deep of heaven,
Flame on flame and wing on wing.

THE MAN WHO DREAMED OF FAERYLAND

He stood among a crowd at Drumahair;
His heart hung all upon a silken dress,
And he had known at last some tenderness,
Before earth made of him her sleepy care;
But when a man poured fish into a pile,
It seemed they raised their little silver heads,
And sang how day a Druid twilight sheds
Upon a dim, green, well-beloved isle,
Where people love beside star-laden seas;
How Time may never mar their faery vows
Under the woven roofs of quicken boughs:
The singing shook him out of his new ease.

He wandered by the sands of Lisadill;
His mind ran all on money cares and fears,
And he had known at last some prudent years
Before they heaped his grave under the hill;
But while he passed before a plashy place,
A lug-worm with its gray and muddy mouth
Sang how somewhere to north or west or south
There dwelt a gay, exulting, gentle race;
And how beneath those three times blessed skies
A Danaan fruitage makes a shower of moons,
And as it falls awakens leafy tunes:
And at that singing he was no more wise.

He mused beside the well of Scanavin,
He mused upon his mockers: without fail
His sudden vengeance were a country tale,
Now that deep earth has drunk his body in;
But one small knot-grass growing by the pool

Told where, ah, little, all-unneeded voice!
Old Silence bids a lonely folk rejoice,
And chaplet their calm brows with leafage cool;
And how, when fades the sea-strewn rose of day,
A gentle feeling wraps them like a fleece,
And all their trouble dies into its peace:
The tale drove his fine angry mood away.

He slept under the hill of Lugnagall;
And might have known at last unhaunted sleep
Under that cold and vapour-turbaned steep,
Now that old earth had taken man and all:
Were not the worms that spired about his bones
A-telling with their low and reedy cry,
Of how God leans His hands out of the sky,
To bless that isle with honey in His tones;
That none may feel the power of squall and wave,
And no one any leaf-crowned dancer miss
Until He burn up Nature with a kiss:
The man has found no comfort in the grave.

THE TWO TREES

Beloved, gaze in thine own heart,
The holy tree is growing there;
From joy the holy branches start,
And all the trembling flowers they bear.
The changing colours of its fruit
Have dowered the stars with merry light;
The surety of its hidden root
Has planted quiet in the night;
The shaking of its leafy head
Has given the waves their melody,
And made my lips and music wed,
Murmuring a wizard song for thee.
There, through bewildered branches, go
Winged Loves borne on in gentle strife,
Tossing and tossing to and fro
The flaming circle of our life.
When looking on their shaken hair,
And dreaming how they dance and dart,
Thine eyes grow full of tender care:
Beloved, gaze in thine own heart.
Gaze no more in the bitter glass
The demons, with their subtle guile,
Lift up before us when they pass,
Or only gaze a little while;
For there a fatal image grows,
With broken boughs, and blackened leaves,
And roots half hidden under snows
Driven by a storm that ever grieves.
For all things turn to barrenness
In the dim glass the demons hold,
The glass of outer weariness,

Made when God slept in times of old.
There, through the broken branches, go
The ravens of unresting thought;
Peering and flying to and fro,
To see men's souls bartered and bought.
When they are heard upon the wind,
And when they shake their wings; alas!
Thy tender eyes grow all unkind:
Gaze no more in the bitter glass.

TO IRELAND IN THE COMING TIMES

Know, that I would accounted be
True brother of that company,
Who sang to sweeten Ireland's wrong,
Ballad and story, rann and song;
Nor be I any less of them,
Because the red-rose-bordered hem
Of her, whose history began
Before God made the angelic clan,
Trails all about the written page;
For in the world's first blossoming age
The light fall of her flying feet
Made Ireland's heart begin to beat;
And still the starry candles flare
To help her light foot here and there;
And still the thoughts of Ireland brood
Upon her holy quietude.

Nor may I less be counted one
With Davis, Mangan, Ferguson,
Because to him, who ponders well,
My rhymes more than their rhyming tell
Of the dim wisdoms old and deep,
That God gives unto man in sleep.
For the elemental beings go
About my table to and fro.
In flood and fire and clay and wind,
They huddle from man's pondering mind;
Yet he who treads in austere ways
May surely meet their ancient gaze.
Man ever journeys on with them
After the red-rose-bordered hem.

Ah, faeries, dancing under the moon,
A Druid land, a Druid tune!

While still I may, I write for you
The love I lived, the dream I knew.
From our birthday, until we die,
Is but the winking of an eye;
And we, our singing and our love,
The mariners of night above,
And all the wizard things that go
About my table to and fro,
Are passing on to where may be,
In truth's consuming ecstasy,
No place for love and dream at all;
For God goes by with white foot-fall.
I cast my heart into my rhymes,
That you, in the dim coming times,
May know how my heart went with them
After the red-rose-bordered hem.

Postscript: WB Yeats and Today's Political Elite

Previously this book was only available in a kindle version. I have taken the opportunity of a paperback edition to make minor corrections to the text and to add this postscript which has been previously published in my essay collection Orwell, Two Guinea Pigs, A Cat and A Goat and other essays. *I have included the essay, as additional material, because the essay refers to* The Lake of Innifree *and thought it may be of some interest to readers of Yeats.*

Whilst still a young man the young Billy Yeats wrote, a poem called *The Lake Isle of Innisfree* (which appears in his second book of poetry) which contains the lines,

'I will arise and go now, for always night and day

I hear lake water lapping with low sounds by the shore'.

With a gentle mournfulness the poem evokes the dream of leaving, going off somewhere, casting-off one's former self, building a log cabin and finding peace in the purple skied afternoons of a beautiful isle. Yeats was a dreamer and loved the notion of the dream, the dream of nature, in a quiet corner of his beloved Ireland.

I was a pacifist when I was young, then in my late teens and early twenties I dabbled with the notion of revolution, having first read socialist, then revolutionary communist tracts and writings. I imagined most young people sought out such works, eager to see justice brought into the world. Yeats himself followed a similar trajectory, being first the dreaming poet, who then grew into a believer in, if not revolution, certainly revolt and rebellion, and ultimately the overthrow of the English in Ireland.

Recently I had the rare opportunity of seeing the inner workings of the political elite in this country. I spent an afternoon with one of the people that coach and advise the upper apparatchiks of the Tory party. Names dropped included: Ruth Davidson, leader of the Scottish Conservatives, and Sajid Javid, Secretary of State for Business and Trade.

Having listened to my host explain a little of his PR work for the government, I then asked him what the naval photos on the wall of his office where all about. He proudly explained, that he'd *'Sort of been* given *a battleship'*, (a P45 Destroyer, if I recall correctly) or least, he'd been 'given' the honorary role of representing the ship at certain military functions and events.

This was reward for work done for the MOD and is

just the kind of sinecure (though unpaid in this case) that elites like to give one another. For a simple boy, (with a working class background and 'Comp' education) who *knows* this is how things work, it was still an eye-opener.

However, what really struck me was how this gentlemen's son, came in at one point to show off a naval calendar. This boy of seven, was full of pride at having learnt the names and details of the various weaponry and instruments of death that his father was involved with. This young boy will soon be off to boarding school in Oxfordshire and I was struck by the notion that he is quite unlikely to grown into his teens reading Trotsky or feeling the need to go on political demonstrations (quite the reverse).

Nonetheless, whilst this boy was not being brought-up in anything like my social background, I still found, or could see, his youthful sweetness, mixed in with his exuberance and the usual childish extremes of love and aggression. All this reminded me of thoughts I'd had earlier that day, that we are *born* pacifists but through socialisation learnt to be war-like.

I don't deny there is an innate aggression within us and naturally we have moments or days when we are argumentative and ornery. The Native American would fight his neighbour when necessary but mostly aggression was expressed and released by traditional rites of passage, which actually *weren't* primarily about war. It was the more technologically developed, 'civilised', European invader that introduced the gun to the Americas, and went on to commit genocide. Indeed, how could one fight war (war of great, devastating consequence at least) without civilisation?

This is not to condemn civil society, it brings great positives along with its nuclear weapons! My point is that to talk of *nature*, as intrinsically related to war, has always seemed to me the opposite of the truth. The young are inclined to seek out excitement (and risk to life and limb can be part of that) but whether one joins the Navy, to engage in warfare (or climbs mountains instead), is surely about the values one is taught and the specific lifestyle and goals, that one sets out to achieve, based on those values. Does one release more aggression on a rugby or football field, than on the fields of Flanders or in the death valleys of Iraq? Which is the healthier? Which is saner, more imaginative, humane, enjoyable or useful?

William Butler Yeats gradually moved from his youthful, pacific, dreams of peace, to the angers and aggressions of civil strife. Which, I wonder, brought him more happiness, peace and contentment?

It's true, anger is a response to injustice, and the dream of peace can only exist if one is surrounded by a just society or one seeks out a quiet corner away from it all. One's heart and mind and passions swing between the two. How can it be otherwise?

Those who fight hardest for social justice are, more often than not, those who have been damaged most by the unjust; those most willing to guide and direct others to war are usually an elite who have been taught, for a long time, over generations, that somehow it is impossible *not* to do so, it is inevitable, natural and necessary.

War is a betrayal of humanity, it utilises our natural aggression, but civilizes and socializes, and transmutes, this emotional and physical state, into the cold anger of killing; and the disinterestedness in empathy and compassion required in battle.

The speed and rapidity of killing today takes our breath away, it doesn't allow for the rendering of justice, it destroys too quickly for that. It contains no consideration, it is the final judgement. A judgement that allows no argument, no debate.

I have lived my life on the isle of dreams mostly, dipped my toe into the troubled waters of human society and politics only infrequently. Perhaps as a consequence, I still believe in judgement and justice. As long as, they are entwined, bound, restricted, enhanced and tempered by, the notion that there is a great need in this world not to harm or hurt others. 'Others' are after all, essentially and certainly genetically, much like oneself. I will engage in both realms (politics and poetry) but live, I hope, mostly on my isle of dreams, because as Yeats wrote,

'I shall have some peace there, for peace comes dropping slow, Dropping from the veils of the morning to where the crickets sings.'

We are naturally aggressive and naturally full of love but love is the deeper, more complex element within us, and ultimately moves society to greater, gentler and more sublime heights.

Other books by Tim Dalgleish

Playing Macbeth: An Actor's Journey into the Role

'Fantastic insider's account... the author has a splendid voice (not surprising) which enhances the experience. If I did have a complaint it would only be that I was sorry for it to end so soon. I would have loved a longer book, but I still would recommend this book to anyone who loves the language of Shakespeare...' Amazon-Audible customer, USA

'Tim Dalgleish has surpassed himself in this fascinating autobiographical effort to pass on the very essence of the art of theatrical performance to the next generation of actors... The reader embarks on a thrilling journey... This little book is actually too big and monumental to give it the credit due within the constraints of this review, but ... it's essential reading for any actor.'
*****Five Star rating from Readers' Favorite

An actor's fascinating journey through the emotional, physical and intellectual challenges involved in creating the role of one of Shakespeare's darkest and most tragic characters. The book includes a journal, The Golden Notebook, with all the hints, history, exercises, theatrical techniques and anecdotes that an actor needs to play Macbeth. Instructive, empowering and a great read.

The Stones of Mithras: Poems of the Light

A beautiful and evocative poetry collection.

'Thoughtful, mysterious at points and overall a very good read'

****Four Star rating from Readers' Favorite

'If you have the feeling of freedom in your heart you begin to look at all things in the world, cornflowers, cigarettes, smoke, clouds, sky, statues, whatever is nearest to hand or vividly remembered as embodied with, soaked in, painted by, the simple magic of light.'

This thought provoking book is a traveller's tale with unforgettable images of lost and ancient cities especially those of Spain. The poems also talk of the romance of acting Shakespeare, the inspiration of great Art, mythology, architecture and the joy of philosophizing over a cup of coffee, sitting in parks and imagining the exploits of writers and artists that went before, from Marco Polo and Maimonides to Marcuse and Garcia Lorca.

Both titles are available as an Amazon paperback and on Kindle

ABOUT THE AUTHOR & EDITOR

William Butler Yeats (1865-1939) was one of the twentieth century's most striking and enduring poets and also an accomplished playwright and critic. He was co-founder, in 1904, of the Abbey Theatre, in Dublin, which was instrumental in the so called Irish Literary Renaissance, staging plays by Sean O'Casey, JM Synge, Lady Gregory, Yeats himself and many others. He was an Irish Senator for two years and was the first Irishman to win the Nobel Prize in Literature. His early poetry dealt with Irish mythology and the occult but in later he developed a realism which rejected many of his former metaphysical beliefs.

Tim Dalgleish is the author of two volumes of poetry *The Stones of* Mithras and *Penumbra*, numerous plays and a book on acting called *Playing Macbeth: An Actor's Journey into the Role*. He has worked with theatre companies from RAT Theatre to Voices of the Holocaust. He was in the feature film *Finding Fatimah* and *Imagine* a short which received Special Mention at the Marbella International Film Festival. His book *Playing Macbeth* was called by reviewers **'A thrilling journey'**, **'Monumental'** and a **'Fantastic insider's view'**. He regularly narrates audio books and writes a blog *The Farthingstone Chronicles* on his website lookingfortim.com.

Made in United States
North Haven, CT
19 November 2023